Recipes

From the kitchen of:

....

....

....

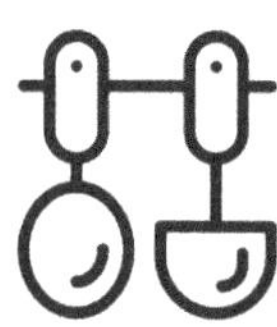

Contents

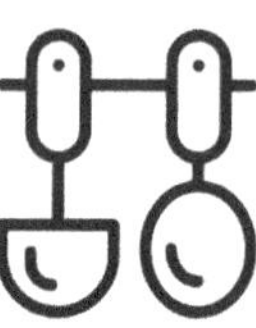

Recipe	Page

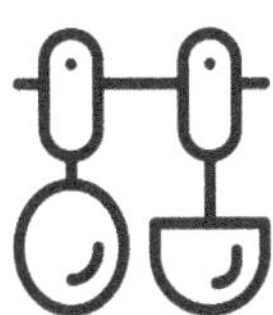

Contents

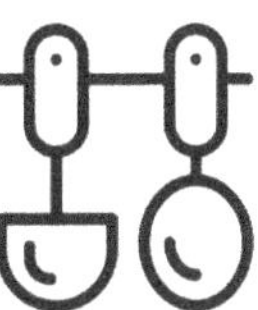

Recipe	Page

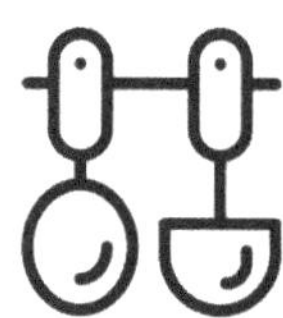

Contents

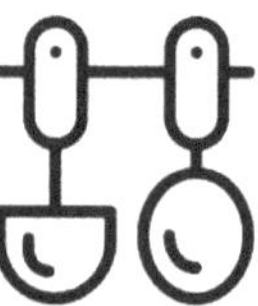

Recipe	Page
....	....
....	....
....	....
....	....
....	....
....	....
....	....
....	....
....	....
....	....
....	....
....	....
....	....
....	....
....	....
....	....
....	....
....	....
....	....
....	....

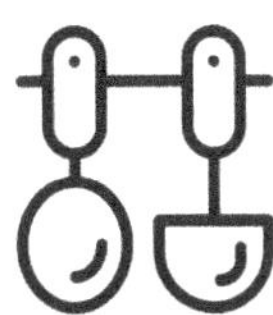

Contents

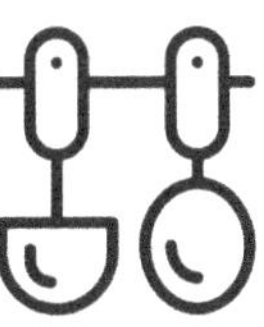

Recipe	Page
....	....
....	....
....	....
....	....
....	....
....	....
....	....
....	....
....	....
....	....
....	....
....	....
....	....
....	....
....	....
....	....
....	....
....	....
....	....
....	....

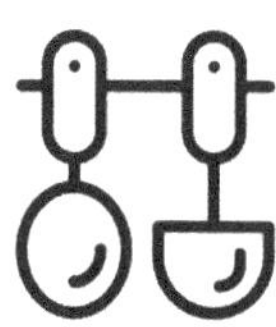

Contents

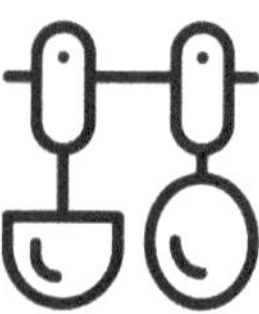

Recipe	Page

Recipe

What's cookin': ....

Servings: .... Cook time: ....

Instructions

Ingredients

Notes

Recipe

What's cookin': ....

Servings: .... **Cook time:** ....

Instructions

....
....
....
....
....
....
....
....
....
....
....
....
....
....
....
....

Ingredients

....	....
....	....
....	....
....	....
....	....
....	....
....	....
....	....
....	....

Notes

....
....
....
....
....

Recipe

What's cookin': ....

Servings: .... Cook time: ....

Instructions

Ingredients

Notes

Recipe

What's cookin': ....

Servings: .... Cook time: ....

Instructions

Ingredients

Notes

Recipe

What's cookin': ....

Servings: .... **Cook time:** ....

Instructions

Ingredients

Notes

Recipe

What's cookin': ....

Servings: .... **Cook time:** ....

Instructions

Ingredients

Notes

Recipe

What's cookin': ....

Servings: .... Cook time: ....

Instructions

Ingredients

Notes

Recipe

What's cookin': ....

Servings: .... Cook time: ....

Instructions

Ingredients

Notes

Recipe

What's cookin':

Servings:

Cook time:

Instructions

Ingredients

Notes

Recipe

What's cookin':

Servings:

Cook time:

Instructions

Ingredients

Notes

Recipe

What's cookin': ....

Servings: .... Cook time: ....

Instructions

Ingredients

Notes

Recipe

What's cookin':

Servings: Cook time:

Instructions

Ingredients

Notes

Recipe

What's cookin':

Servings:

Cook time:

Instructions

Ingredients

Notes

Recipe

What's cookin': ....

Servings: ....

Cook time: ....

Instructions

Ingredients

Notes

Recipe

What's cookin': ....

Servings: ....   Cook time: ....

Instructions

Ingredients

Notes

Recipe

What's cookin': ....

Servings: .... Cook time: ....

Instructions

Ingredients

Notes

Recipe

What's cookin': ....

Servings: .... Cook time: ....

Instructions

Ingredients

Notes

Recipe

What's cookin': ....

Servings: .... **Cook time:** ....

Instructions

Ingredients

Notes

Recipe

What's cookin': ....

Servings: .... Cook time: ....

Instructions

Ingredients

Notes

Recipe

What's cookin':

Servings: Cook time:

Instructions

Ingredients

Notes

Recipe

What's cookin': ....

Servings: .... Cook time: ....

Instructions

Ingredients

Notes

Recipe

What's cookin': ....

Servings: .... Cook time: ....

Instructions

Ingredients

Notes

Recipe

What's cookin':

Servings:

Cook time:

Instructions

Ingredients

Notes

Recipe

What's cookin': ....

Servings: ....   Cook time: ....

Instructions

Ingredients

Notes

Recipe

What's cookin':

Servings:

Cook time:

Instructions

Ingredients

Notes

Recipe

What's cookin': ....

Servings: .... Cook time: ....

Instructions

Ingredients

Notes

Recipe

What's cookin': ....

Servings: .... Cook time: ....

Instructions

Ingredients

Notes

Recipe

What's cookin': ....

Servings: .... Cook time: ....

Instructions

Ingredients

Notes

Recipe

What's cookin': ....

Servings: .... Cook time: ....

Instructions

Ingredients

Notes

Recipe

What's cookin': ....

Servings: .... Cook time: ....

Instructions

Ingredients

Notes

Recipe

What's cookin':

Servings:

Cook time:

Instructions

Ingredients

Notes

Recipe

What's cookin': ....

Servings: .... **Cook time:** ....

Instructions

Ingredients

Notes

Recipe

What's cookin': ....

Servings: ....   Cook time: ....

Instructions

Ingredients

Notes

Recipe

What's cookin': ....

Servings: ....   Cook time: ....

Instructions	Ingredients

Notes

Recipe

What's cookin': ....

Servings: .... Cook time: ....

Instructions

Ingredients

Notes

Recipe

What's cookin': ....

Servings: .... **Cook time:** ....

Instructions

Ingredients

Notes

Recipe

What's cookin': ....

Servings: .... Cook time: ....

Instructions

Ingredients

Notes

Recipe

What's cookin': ....

Servings: .... **Cook time:** ....

Instructions

Ingredients

Notes

Recipe

What's cookin':

Servings: Cook time:

Instructions

Ingredients

Notes

Recipe

What's cookin': ....

Servings: .... **Cook time:** ....

Instructions

Ingredients

Notes

Recipe

What's cookin':

Servings:

Cook time:

Instructions

Ingredients

Notes

Recipe

What's cookin': ....

Servings: .... Cook time: ....

Instructions

Ingredients

Notes

Recipe

What's cookin': ....

Servings: ....   Cook time: ....

Instructions

Ingredients

Notes

Recipe

What's cookin': ....

Servings: .... Cook time: ....

Instructions

Ingredients

Notes

Recipe

What's cookin': ....

Servings: .... Cook time: ....

Instructions

Ingredients

Notes

Recipe

What's cookin': ....

Servings: .... Cook time: ....

Instructions

Ingredients

Notes

Recipe

What's cookin': ....

Servings: .... Cook time: ....

Instructions

Ingredients

Notes

Recipe

What's cookin': ....

Servings: .... Cook time: ....

Instructions

Ingredients

Notes

Recipe

What's cookin':

Servings:

Cook time:

Instructions

Ingredients

Notes

Recipe

What's cookin': ....

Servings: .... Cook time: ....

Instructions

Ingredients

Notes

Recipe

What's cookin': ....

Servings: .... **Cook time:** ....

Instructions

Ingredients

Notes

Recipe

What's cookin': ....

Servings: .... Cook time: ....

Instructions

Ingredients

Notes

Recipe

What's cookin': ....

Servings: ....

Cook time: ....

Instructions

Ingredients

Notes

Recipe

What's cookin': ....

Servings: .... **Cook time:** ....

Instructions

Ingredients

Notes

Recipe

What's cookin': ....

Servings: .... Cook time: ....

Instructions

Ingredients

Notes

Recipe

What's cookin': ....

Servings: .... Cook time: ....

Instructions

Ingredients

Notes

Recipe

What's cookin': ....

Servings: .... Cook time: ....

Instructions

Ingredients

Notes

Recipe

What's cookin': ....

Servings: .... Cook time: ....

Instructions

Ingredients

Notes

Recipe

What's cookin':

Servings:

Cook time:

Instructions

Ingredients

Notes

Recipe

What's cookin': ....

Servings: .... Cook time: ....

Instructions

Ingredients

Notes

Recipe

What's cookin':

Servings:

Cook time:

Instructions

Ingredients

Notes

Recipe

What's cookin': ....

Servings: .... Cook time: ....

Instructions

Ingredients

Notes

Recipe

What's cookin': ....

Servings: .... Cook time: ....

Instructions

Ingredients

Notes

Recipe

What's cookin':

Servings: Cook time:

Instructions

Ingredients

Notes

Recipe

What's cookin':

Servings:

Cook time:

Instructions

Ingredients

Notes

Recipe

What's cookin': ....

Servings: .... Cook time: ....

Instructions

Ingredients

Notes

Recipe

What's cookin': ....

Servings: .... Cook time: ....

Instructions

Ingredients

Notes

Recipe

What's cookin': ....

Servings: .... Cook time: ....

Instructions

Ingredients

Notes

Recipe

What's cookin': ....

Servings: .... Cook time: ....

Instructions

Ingredients

Notes

Recipe

What's cookin': ....

Servings: .... **Cook time:** ....

Instructions

....
....
....
....
....
....
....
....
....
....
....
....
....
....
....
....

Ingredients

....
....
....
....
....
....
....
....
....

Notes

....
....
....
....
....

Recipe

What's cookin': ....

Servings: .... **Cook time:** ....

Instructions

Ingredients

Notes

Recipe

What's cookin': ....

Servings: .... Cook time: ....

Instructions

Ingredients

Notes

Recipe

What's cookin': ....

Servings: .... Cook time: ....

Instructions

Ingredients

Notes

Recipe

What's cookin': ....

Servings: .... **Cook time:** ....

Instructions

....
....
....
....
....
....
....
....
....
....
....
....
....
....
....
....

Ingredients

....	....
....	....
....	....
....	....
....	....
....	....
....	....
....	....
....	....

Notes

....
....
....
....
....

Recipe

What's cookin': ....

Servings: .... Cook time: ....

Instructions

Ingredients

Notes

Recipe

What's cookin':

Servings: Cook time:

Instructions

Ingredients

Notes

Recipe

What's cookin': ....

Servings: .... Cook time: ....

Instructions

Ingredients

Notes

Recipe

What's cookin': ....

Servings: .... Cook time: ....

Instructions

Ingredients

Notes

Recipe

What's cookin': ....

Servings: .... Cook time: ....

Instructions

Ingredients

Notes

Recipe

What's cookin': ....

Servings: .... Cook time: ....

Instructions

Ingredients

Notes

Recipe

What's cookin': ....

Servings: ....   Cook time: ....

Instructions

Ingredients

Notes

Recipe

What's cookin': ....

Servings: ....   Cook time: ....

Instructions

Ingredients

Notes

Recipe

What's cookin': ....

Servings: .... **Cook time:** ....

Instructions

Ingredients

Notes

Recipe

What's cookin': ....

Servings: .... Cook time: ....

Instructions

Ingredients

Notes

Recipe

What's cookin': ....

Servings: .... Cook time: ....

Instructions

Ingredients

Notes

Recipe

What's cookin': ....

Servings: .... Cook time: ....

Instructions

Ingredients

Notes

Recipe

What's cookin':

Servings: Cook time:

Instructions

Ingredients

Notes

Recipe

What's cookin': ....

Servings: .... Cook time: ....

Instructions

Ingredients

Notes

Recipe

What's cookin': ....

Servings: .... Cook time: ....

Instructions

Ingredients

Notes

Recipe

What's cookin': ....

Servings: .... **Cook time:** ....

Instructions

Ingredients

Notes

Recipe

What's cookin': ....

Servings: .... Cook time: ....

Instructions

Ingredients

Notes

Recipe

What's cookin': ....

Servings: .... Cook time: ....

Instructions

Ingredients

Notes

Recipe

What's cookin': ....

Servings: ....   Cook time: ....

Instructions

Ingredients

Notes

Recipe

What's cookin': ....

Servings: ....   Cook time: ....

Instructions

Ingredients

Notes

Recipe

What's cookin': ....

Servings: .... Cook time: ....

Instructions

Ingredients

Notes

Recipe

What's cookin': ....

Servings: .... **Cook time:** ....

Instructions

Ingredients

Notes

Recipe

What's cookin': ....

Servings: .... Cook time: ....

Instructions

Ingredients

Notes

Recipe

What's cookin': ....

Servings: .... Cook time: ....

Instructions

Ingredients

Notes

Recipe

What's cookin': ....

Servings: ....   Cook time: ....

Instructions

Ingredients

Notes

Recipe

What's cookin': ....

Servings: .... **Cook time:** ....

Instructions

Ingredients

Notes

www.ingramcontent.com/pod-product-compliance
Lightning Source LLC
Chambersburg PA
CBHW041915130726
48007CB00015B/184